SETTING

BOUNDARIES

WITH YOUR

AFRICAN-AMERICAN

SON

8 Practical Steps to Take Control of Your Life

Dr. Leslie

Copyright

Copyright © 2018 by Dr. Leslie

Published 2018

ISBN-13: 9781723905506

DISCLAIMER

Brand and product names are trademarks or registered trademarks of their respective owners.

Cover Design: Canva Stock Photo

Editing: Danielle Hamilton

Author's photo courtesy of Chau High

DEDICATION

Before I knew I had a message…

Before I knew I wanted to start a movement with my message…

There was a reason.

That reason, my reason for talking about something that everyone knows but nobody is really talking about in this manner, is for the liberation of every Mother and her Son in hopes that their lives will be forever changed as a result of understanding their relationship because of the strategies and support received as a result of reading this book.

Table of Contents

Introduction

A bookinar can mean many things to different people, but much like a seminar or webinar, it involves a group of people that come together to receive what is deemed as valuable information. One Monday evening, I had my first bookinar at 7:00 p.m. I gave my daughter, Kiara, the responsibility of getting some people on the call to listen in. Once I gave her the responsibility, I did not worry about it. She is good about things like that. My concern was deciding which one of the chapters I was going to read.

The purpose of the bookinar was to get people excited about my book and to get valuable feedback from them so that I could make improvements. About 15 minutes prior to the bookinar, I decided to read, what I thought, might be considered a controversial chapter. I wanted to know if it should even be a part of the book. That question was answered immediately after the bookinar. During the bookinar, I only read that chapter. I did not accept any questions or comments during the call. The listeners were emailed a 5 question survey to complete and email right back, and most of them did. The decision to keep that chapter was unanimous! I received several phone calls immediately after the bookinar from women who were grateful to have listened in and be a part of the bookinar.

The one question that I was asked over and over was, "Now what?" The feedback said they needed and wanted more. They needed solutions! Many of the women that participated on the call were able to find themselves somewhere in what I had read and said that they knew they had to change. In fact, they needed to change for the sake of their own personal peace and for their Son…even if their Son was a grown man already. It is never too late to change. That is when I decided to extract that specific chapter from the book and make it a book of its own. I decided to make it a self-help book particularly for Black women raising Black Sons, but anybody can use these strategies.

Is This Book for You?

This book is for Black Mothers that feel they did everything they could for their Son and they expected him to grow into a healthy, happy, successful young man, but he hasn't, at least not yet - and even though these problems didn't just start, the fact that they threaten your peace of mind, your health, your freedom, your relationship with your husband/boyfriend, and/or your job or other family relationships, you've got to do something! If you are sick and tired of being sick and tired, then you need to read every word in this book and take it seriously because your life is at stake. You need to read it as if your life depends on it because it does. I don't know, perhaps it is the red busted eye vessels in each of your eyes, perhaps it is the constant migraine headaches that you have day after day or the fact that you have not had any sleep the last few nights worrying about your Son. Something has to give. Whether the process is gradual or unexpected, a sudden lack of wise choices, financial responsibility, and decent friendships, the internal reaction is the same-HARD! It is hard because you are trying to figure out what went wrong when you had good intentions for your Son. You did the best you could with what you knew and it gives you a feeling of betrayal. You have forgiven him over and over again, but the cycle of pain in your heart continues as time after time your Son accepts your help but promises this is the last time he will need your assistance, then turns around and does the same thing again, and there was no one else there to rescue him, but you. It is costing you too much not to take steps to solve this problem. You want your Son to be happy on his own, yet you may live in fear of not doing enough to help him. This is not easy, because you feel that because you are his Mother, it is your responsibility to take care of him and meet his needs...even if he is all grown up or refuses to grow up. It is with compassion and perspective that I offer life-affirming messages to those of you who are still trying to "fix" your Son. I want to show you how to separate from his problems without separating from him, and how to be a positive force in his life while being able to move on with your own life. Your Son may be in his teens, twenties, thirties, forties or older, but you now realize that it is you he calls for every financial and emotional problem that he

8

has, and you go running to help in utter frustration the entire way. You fuss at him, but you still give him what he needs because you feel that you are helping him. You wonder what he will do without you. You are tired of being disappointed and caught up in your Son's cycle of destructive behavior as if you made the bad decision. You are motivated to help him have the best chance of being happy and successful in life but you secretly wonder if you are doing too much and may be hurting him. Some people may have told you that you do too much for your Son, but what if they are wrong. He is not their Son, he's yours. You really don't want him to struggle like you did. You want to make life easy for him so that he does not have to worry about certain things and can focus on being great at what he does or doing well in school.

Deep down inside, you know that your Son's problems are ruining your relationships, your health, your freedom, your job, your peace of mind, and your overall well-being. You are losing sleep wondering what you are going to do and how you are going to stop responding to his needs and yes, sometimes, foolishness. You know you need to stop. And for those of you who are reading this who have young boys who are causing you grief, this book is for you too, because young grief becomes old grief. When I see little boys, 2, 3, and 4 years old acting up, I will say with a smile, *better get a hold of that, it doesn't get better.* Sometimes I get the feeling that Mom has no clue what she is in for. It is easier and best to handle behavior challenges when your Son is small. Some of the most intelligent, handsome, articulate, and charismatic young Black men that I have worked with are also some of the most foolish, dangerous, frightening, and misguided individuals I have ever met.

In some cases, your Son has lost sight of his own goals, has a horrible work ethic, and bounces around from career to career. Does your Son have less than perfect character? Perhaps your Son has no drive or ambition and has a sense of entitlement? If so, you need to read this book from cover to cover. This book will show you the way by helping you see how you got to this place and how you can get on the road to your peace of mind by being real with yourself and using the practical steps to help you set boundaries with your Son with no love lost.

Chapter One: My Story

How I Came to Understand This Problem

I want to tell you how I came to understand this problem for myself. I started to really connect the dots of all of my experiences in 2009. That is when I began to notice there was a distinct difference between how boys responded to Mothers and how they responded to their Fathers. When working with African-American children in general, you tend to see Mothers far more than you see Fathers, especially if you work in a Title I school or in a low income school that primarily serves Black children.

One of the most prominent scenarios that comes to mind when I think of examples of how I came to understand the problem takes me back to when I worked as Instructional Liaison Specialist in the public school system in 2001. I can remember that time frame well because I remember stopping in the office area watching airplanes run into the twin towers in New York shortly before a meeting.

I have seen thousands of women faced with the challenges associated with raising Black boys, and many are doing the best that they can. The last several years have been the worst that I have seen and experienced, and I am starting to encounter more people who want to have this conversation. I have found that married women are struggling with this problem just as much as single women. Some women may read this book and think... *Oh, no, not me...I don't play that.* I hear that too. A lot! And the Mother that says that usually has one of the worst Sons.

Let me tell you what I keep seeing over and over again with the parents that I work with…not every now and then, but over and over again. Remember that this is a "type" of Son. There are many characteristics that this Son may have, but the way it impacts or affects Mom is the same at some point in her life.

Mom thinks her Son is the most precious thing walking on the universe. She keeps him neat and tidy. She keeps his hair nicely cut. He may dress neat or he may be a slob. This boy may not brush his teeth or comb his hair in the morning. This boy is manipulative. This boy is sneaky. This boy lies to his Mom because he knows that he can get away with it. Over the years, he has become a mastermind at manipulating her. When I say over the years, he may be so smart that he learns how to master manipulate Mom by age two. This boy tells his Mom how he is the victim of everything, and she gets upset over the thought of anybody trying to do something or tell her something wrong about her Son or to her Son. This boy, now, young man, is either syrupy sweet towards his Mom or just downright disrespectful towards her OR rebellious in a subtle way meaning he does not show blatant disrespect, but he will have an attitude towards her and simply not do what she asks of him, give her a kiss on the cheek, then say I'm sorry. This type of Son has many faces. Consequently, he has a way of controlling her through manipulation. When the boy is young, Mom thinks it is cute. When he gets older and has truly mastered her behavior, it is no longer cute. Some Mothers keep telling themselves that perhaps this is only a phase that he is going through because she keeps telling herself that he is a good kid. He has challenges accepting responsibility for his actions or does not take part in making his home situation better to include himself and everyone else that lives in the house. He looks for Mom to do it, and she does. She takes the trash out while he sits and plays video games, and he watches his Mom while she is doing it, but he acts as if he does not see her. He has little sense of responsibility, and she consciously or subconsciously makes excuses for him because she loves him so much, but then, we have to question how love is defined in this situation.

At the school I founded, Solid Foundation, our students have jobs so we can always tell who does housework or chores at home. Many of the older boys do not know how to sweep a floor, close a trash bag, or take out the trash and will run if asked to do it.

On the contrary, there are some boys that you can tell that they have responsibilities at home because they love to help out at school, and they are good at it. Some boys are very accommodating towards female teachers. Whenever they see us with bags in our hands, they will come and take our bags and help us carry them. That's the Son whose Mother has taught him when she gets home that they better help her unload the car and put the groceries in the house. Overall, you can tell that the boy that exhibits those behaviors is not lazy and is accustomed to doing work. In many cases, we already know how the Mother is based on the Son's actions and reactions at school.

Remember, we work with the children we serve about 7 hours of the day. In some instances, we hear Mothers say that they wished their Son did work at home like he does at school. We have also had Mothers whose Son complained to her about him having to do chores at school, and as a result, we were approached by that Mother saying that he should not have to help us clean the school.

I have also come to recognize that whereas some boys will work for us at school, many will not work for their Mothers because they know their Mothers do not believe that they can do it. This can be a seemingly small task such as setting the house alarm or being at home alone for an hour or two in the 11th or 12th grade. The young man may be capable, but somewhere along the way, he lost his Mother's trust, so she babies him into believing that he cannot do what she said he cannot do. But he can do it. We see it everyday.

These groups of young men are going to find it difficult to thrive in society or provide a stable financial existence for themselves and for their families OR they will be on that Mother's couch at age 40 because that is what she cultivated in him all of his life. I'm not telling you what I think, I am telling you what I know. I have had personal conversations with many of my parents about this over the years and have helped many women to stop toxic behavior with their Sons because it hurts me when I see this. Ultimately, I want our young men to become productive citizens in society without their Mothers hindering their progress towards becoming a man.

Me and one of my childhood friends, who is also an educator, had a recent conversation about our children. We both agreed that it is important to raise children as if you are dying. That conversation was held in detail after her 53 year old sister dropped dead unexpectedly. Behind she left two teenage boys ages 16 and 19 but mentally, they were

12 and 14. Their Mother did everything for them. Now they were Motherless and the Father was in their life but not very active. They knew who he was but he did not step up to the plate as one would have expected or *maybe he did.* Nevertheless, the family was left to decide who was going to take care of these grown boys? Nobody wanted to do it because they looked like men, talked like men, they ate like men, and in a certain kind of way, wanted to be men. They were just extremely immature in their thoughts and level of responsibility. Needless to say, they had to grow up continuing to live in the home of their deceased Mother. Just the two of them, the blind leading the blind. I don't know if their Mother thought she was going to live a long time, or at least until they were old enough to take care of themselves. So, when she died, guess what happened? Those immature boys had no other options. They now had to figure out life for themselves without anyone to rescue them when they made mistakes. I want to add that they gave their Mother a hard time while she was living. They did not appreciate her. I often wonder if my friend's sister had lived like she was dying would she have raised her

Son's as if she may not be there one day. I wonder what she would have done differently?

Anonymous Email I Wrote to a Parent

Hi Ms. xxxx I pray all is well with you. I am writing because I want to share my heart and my concerns with you regarding your Son. I have NEVER received as many negative emails and text messages in my whole career of education as I have received from you within the last 4 weeks regarding xxxxxxx and other students. As I stated in your parent conference, I like xxxxx and I think he is a smart child. Nevertheless, I am concerned about his ability to tell you things and you believe them enough to write a full page negative response. I have genuinely grown to like you as a parent and as a Woman of God. However, my 25 years of experience in dealing with boys and their Mothers tells me to share with you that you may want to leave some room for xxxxx to grow up and learn how to deal with issues with his peers on his own because many of the issues are started by xxxxx. There is no way that one kid can have these many altercations with other students unless

19

something else is wrong. When dealing with children from all walks of life, you have to take the good with the bad. We work hard to be patient with our children and teach them from their mistakes. Sometimes that learning process takes longer than other times. Nevertheless, we try to hang in there as long as we can and do the best that we can. Lastly, if this does not work, you may want to consider homeschooling or joining a homeschool group for xxxxxx. I would hate to lose him, but I want what is best for him just like you.

I had never written a letter like that before to a parent, but enough was enough. I had to do something. I knew at that point the Son was not the problem, the Mother was the problem. The Son manipulated his Mother so much at such a young age, that I couldn't believe it. I considered him to be a Mastermind of Manipulation. I will keep the rest to myself.

Accessory to the Crime

I remember working in the public school setting, in an administrative capacity, before I learned how to be the professional lady that I am today. It was actually this situation that taught me how to be cool, calm, and collected when dealing with parents.

Two little third grade boys were caught in someone's classroom throughout the morning stealing candy out of a teacher's drawer.

First of all, they had to case out the place and come up with a game plan. They watched the teacher time and time again go into the drawer to provide treats for her students, so they knew exactly where the goods were. Somehow, they escaped from the common meeting area, the gym, which is where students were held after they ate breakfast. Staff members were stationed along the hallways to prevent students wandering the halls in the morning as a safety precaution. Well, these two students were caught, and this became a very serious matter to me. If you work with children and are serious about their future, things that may be small to other people are big to you. Someone else may have thought, *they are only 7/8 years old*. But I saw them as two 18-year old boys stealing a car! We contacted the parents, who were single parents by the way. I remember meeting with one of the parents in particular. After we told her what had happened, she asked? *"DID YOU ACTUALLY SEE HIS HAND IN THE DRAWER TAKING THE CANDY?"* She said it bold and with an attitude...head shaking, neck rolling, lips puckered, hand in the air with fingers pointed and moving with her every word. Remember there were two boys. This was the Mother of the boy who was *with* the boy that was actually stealing the candy. I jumped out of my seat and found myself doing the same thing that she was doing, speaking boldly, with an attitude...head shaking, neck rolling, lips puckered, hand in the air with fingers pointed and moving with my every word. The School Principal that I worked with at the time gave me the eye and shook his head informing me to calm down. I remember saying, *"MA'AM! HE WAS AN ACCESSORY TO THE CRIME! IF HE WAS IN A STORE*

THEY WOULD TAKE HIM TO JAILLLLLL! AN ACCESSORY IS CHARGED JUST AS MUCH AS THE PERSON WHO DID IT." After the meeting when the school principal and I met to debrief what had happened, he told me to never let any parent get me so riled up that they take me out of my character. He said in a joking voice, *"I have never seen you like that, you were going off on that lady."* I changed my ways after that. In this field, you are not going to agree with every parent, but you have to respect them and their decisions and their way of thinking as to how they are going to raise or discipline their child. Consequently, everyone that was in the meeting that day agreed that boy would be in jail one day simply because his Mother defended him even when she knew in her heart her Son was wrong as two left shoes.

I often see a type of silent resentment that some boys develop towards their Mothers. I see it more often than I care to admit. Yes, they love their Mother, but in the eyes of some boys, as they get older, I see a type of quiet desperation and cry for help. I think deep down inside, they want their Mother to let them grow up and be a man because the man is trying to break through the little boy inside who is crying out. The man is screaming out loudly trying to get out, but many won't scream out loud or in public at their Mother, and some will. Mom is the only real support that they truly have, in many cases. Instead, what I see through my lenses as a teacher, mentor, support, an inspiration, and the like with the countless young men that have come through the Solid Foundation path, is rebellion. As a result, we have 30, 40, and 50 year old grown boys still living at home because their Moms treated them like she never wanted them to leave. A vicious cycle is created that before long they are so dependent on the money and support received from their Mother that they can't fathom surviving financially on their own. They turn into spoiled, often depressed, adult children. And many Mothers wonder where they went wrong. It started when they stole the candy out of the teacher's desk drawer.

Boys transitioning to Men have their own way of reading their Mothers and Mothers need a different way to provide a tough love shield against manipulation. It is usually a man. A real man can help bring balance to that situation if she allows him.

One other example that I remember vividly is of a young man who was late to school almost every single day. He was either late or he did not come. This young man was so smart, brilliant as a matter and fact. As it got closer for him to graduate from Solid Foundation, I became more concerned about how he would function after he graduated. What would he do? He had the intelligence but seemingly lacked the responsibility to hold a job or go to college and attend classes on his own. I had a conversation with his Mom who placed most of the blame on him staying up all night and not wanting to get up in the morning. We decided that we would go and pick him up for school every morning. The young man agreed and said he would be ready. Do you know that young man was outside rain or shine, on time every morning? Ready. What would you think after that?

I had a conversation, several actually, with his Mother because obviously, she was the problem. In addition to that, this young man had the hardest time making a decision as to which college he was going to attend after graduation. What was the problem? We took our students to visit various college campuses in Atlanta. He took the ASVAB and scored very high. What was the problem? Graduation came and went. Before graduation, I had personal conversations with him and his Mother about what he was going to do. The fact that he couldn't make a decision bothered me so much that I decided to start having one on one conversations with him. I noticed a difference in him during the one on one conversations as opposed to the ones with his Mother. He wanted to be human. He wanted to be talked to and not talked at. His Mother fussed and fussed about his indecisiveness and shouted about what she was tired of dealing with as far as he was concerned. She even told me what his Grandmother wanted him to do. You see, he was being raised by his Grandmother and his Mother. By now, the summer was coming to a close. I had not spoken to the young man, but I did not want him to not attend college, he was too smart. I thought about his future daily. He had too much to offer the world.

I received a call that his Grandmother was in the hospital so I made sure I went to see her because I love this lady. I sat with her for about 45 minutes and we talked about everything. I knew that she had made many sacrifices for her Grandson and only wanted the best for him. So, near the end of our conversation, I asked her about her Grandson. She answered. I asked her what she wanted him to do next. Grandma had all the power and authority. She said I want him to go to school, he needs to go to somebody's school. I told her that I got it from here. That is all I needed to hear.

I called the young man's Mom a couple of days after that to talk to her about something else. Her Son was sitting next to her in the car. She started yelling and fussing at him in the car and said that he said he was not going to college until the Spring and proceeded to tell me why. I couldn't even think of him wasting time at home and not going to college or doing something productive with his life. I did not want him to get complacent. Mom fussed as she got out of the car and handed her Son the phone because she had to run into a building real quick. While she was in the car and asked him questions, his answers or responses were lifeless, carefree, full of doubt and apathy. After she got out of the car and I started talking to him without her being there, it was as if a dying flower in a pot of dirt had just received water. During our conversation, I could hear hope in his voice. He confirmed with me that he wanted to go to college but could not see how it could happen since he waited so long. Since he now had hope, he then whispered to me even though he was the only person in the car and asked, *"will I be able to stay on campus if I go to college?"* I answered to him, *"yes."* I told him that we were going to have to work hard to find a college for him because most of the deadlines had passed. I continued by telling him that he was going to have to be more responsible by getting up in the mornings on his own and finding a job as well. He assured me that he wanted to work. We started looking online at that moment. Here is what the young man said to me in the most humble tone of voice, *"I will be fine in college. I can get up on my own, too. The only reason I sleep all day and stay up all night is because that is the only time I can get some peace while everyone else is sleeping."* My eyes got full for that moment, and I knew he was going to be ok. He did not say it in a disrespectful manner, he was talking to me at that moment in time like he knew that I could and would help him and like I was his last hope. The one thing that I knew and have always known is that He needed to get away from his Mother, quickly. That was a Tuesday, his Mother was driving him to college that Friday. We pulled it off. I want to cry right now. With God, all things are possible to him that believe.

I have to hand it to his Mom, she followed all instructions and we worked together to get him there not even fully knowing if they had a bed for him. His Mother just needed guidance. Now she needs guidance to leave him alone and let him grow up and be a man while he is away at school.

These are just a few of the stories that have helped me to get on my soul's path and walk in my gifts. There is much more to those stories to be told and many more stories to tell. It is also the fact that women trust me and ask me for help all the time. This is what I was born to do, it seems as if I am a magnet for women that need help with their Sons. I want to help Black women get a better hold on their Sons at an early age so that she can have a happier life minimizing the pitfalls, frustration, and anxiety of dealing with a lazy, codependent Son who refuses to do anything with his life except drain the life out of her.

In the event that we don't catch it early, I also want to help Black women who thought their Son's behavior was cute when they were young, but now are suffering the consequences by allowing his behavior patterns and bad decisions threaten her peace of mind, her health, her freedom, her relationships, and her job. We relate to the type of student they are today to the type of man they will be tomorrow.

I want to help Black Mothers figure this out because it will help the job of educators. Educators see it all. We deal with your Son's behavior problems, his bad decisions, and his lack of disrespect and we get tired of dealing with it, even when he disrespects you and you make excuses for him. That alone gives me a vested interest in helping Black women so that we can ultimately help Black men.

Chapter Two: The Big Solution

A Success Story

Before you begin to change your Son, it is you, Mom, whose behavior needs to change. Yes, you!

As a Mother, naturally you want to give your Son what he wants because God designed us to be givers. It hurts us when we cannot give our Son what he wants, and it does not change when they are adults. But you cannot expect your Son to become independent and confident in himself if you keep doing everything for him. You may want his behavior to change, but the change must start with you. One of my clients who is also a very good friend of mine started telling me about a situation with her oldest Son who was about 2 years old when she got a divorce. By the time her oldest Son was 5 years old, she gave him almost everything he wanted because she was overcompensating for his Father not being there, and she felt guilty that his Father was not there. She was now in her 2nd marriage and they had a child together, therefore, her oldest Son sometimes felt more like an outsider from her, her husband, and her younger Son, the offspring of her and her 2nd husband. I must add that her 2nd husband had been around since her oldest Son was 5 and practically raised her Son like he was his own child. Nevertheless, deep down inside, my client would harbor negative feelings, subconsciously, when it was time for the Stepfather to discipline her Son knowing that he was not his real Father. I am sure there was a lot of *"you're not my real Father!"* And that would, of course, put my client and her husband at odds.

After a huge blow up with her Son, my client put her oldest Son out of the house again. This time he really had to grow up and get himself together. Days turned into weeks and weeks turned into months in which she and her Son did not speak. I don't think she expected it to go as long as it did, but the *breakup* affected her health very much even though she worked out often. She looked great on the outside but was slowly dying on the inside.

During one of our sessions, after hearing all of the strategies and trying to figure out how to move forward with her life and get her peace back, her main question was "how do I keep moving when he is all I think about? I am wondering how he is doing. He doesn't have a job and I am wondering if I should give him his car so that maybe if he got a job he would have a way to get back and forth to work. I don't know where he is or how he is doing. What do I do in the meantime while I am waiting?" The question I thought is waiting on what? Waiting on him to come to his senses and come back and apologize? Waiting on him to say he wanted to come back home? Waiting on what? She was in tears as she spoke these words. She also commented that she could not be as heartless and cruel as everyone in the bookinar group told her she should be or as cruel and heartless as others in the group admitted that they had learned to be in order for them to get their peace back from their children. They were not telling her to be cruel and heartless, the group was actually encouraging her to set some boundaries with her Son. I want to add that the women in the group had boys and girls and many had suffered or are suffering with the same exact problems. Nevertheless, I knew as long as she felt that way, I had my work cut out for me, but I was ready for the challenge. I knew right then and there, the solution to her problem as well as with other Black women and their Sons is to educate them and change their belief system and surround them with other women who are going through the same thing.

I knew that I was making headway with this particular client when she called me to tell me that she had spoken to her Son and he told her that he was coming to see her that day. She was excited because she had not seen him since the *breakup*. He only communicated with her indirectly via her youngest Son through nasty text messages. She got more upset with each text message that was shared with her, and her oldest Son knew exactly what he was doing. Nevertheless, she came home and found that her Son had already been there. Her husband had spoken with him. She asked her husband what the visit was like and what he talked about, and he responded by saying, *"same ol stuff, nothing has changed."* My client showed a lot of growth right here by identifying that she was upset at her husband's response. She felt like he should have been a little more sympathetic towards her Son's situation and happy that he came to the house. Well, her husband put 2 and 2 together and said that he was manipulating his way to go on the family cruise that they were scheduled to go on the next day. He was supposed to be going with them, but they decided not to take him due to his lack of respect towards everyone in the house along with the lifestyle that was afforded to him. He had already wrecked three (3) cars that they replaced for him. What next? My client was sad that she missed his visit and wondered when she would be able to see him again. Her gut wanted to ask him back and say *"come home! Let's stop all of this."* I let her talk out how she felt. Her number one question to me was *"do you think I am being manipulated by him?"* I said, *"absolutely!"* Her voice began to rise and she asked me how did I see it as manipulation. I told her. She tried to make herself understand but instead, she stopped trying to rationalize and took my word. I told her not to call him back. (This is the time when Coaching is very important. You need someone to help see you through your blind spots). This is not the time to get weak and cave in. I told her that God carefully orchestrated his visit so that she wouldn't be there. She would have never missed that visit had she known exactly what time he was coming. She had only gone out for a short time, but it was enough time for him to come and go. Funny thing, her husband did not call her on her cell phone to let her know that her Son had arrived. What I have found is that we may see this as being a socioeconomic problem, but many of the women that I Coach are educated, professional Black women. They are doctors, attorneys, educators, entrepreneurs and other professionals who love their Sons and set out on a path to give them what they never had. Many of them did not want their Son to struggle like they did. But what we have found is, now you have another problem. *Entitlement.* Entitlement comes with manipulation whether the child is spoiled and comes from a family that has or from a family that has not. Even in all of their strength, it can be difficult for the Black Mother to see through their Son's manipulation. Black Mothers that are continuously manipulated by their Black Sons need intervention, and they need to be honest with themselves or maybe somebody just needs to be honest with them. That is where I come in. You can't just tell them that they are being manipulated by their Son, even if they know it. Usually, I work to build trust with my clients so that they trust me enough for me to say to them, "Stop it before you let him kill you!" That usually wakes them up, and believe me, I say it more than I'd like to.

Raising Daughters and Nurturing Our Black Sons
It has been my experience while working in public and private schools to see that it is evident that many Black Mothers raise their Daughters and nurture their Sons. This tendency of parenting is most often seen amongst populations with lesser economic resources, such as the Black community, but not always. I see it over and over and it makes me really think about where we are as a culture of parenting Black boys. In my opinion, Black women need extra help in raising their Black Sons. I have a Black Son who is mild mannered and compliant, for the most part, and it can still be a struggle for me. Thank God for the positive Black men in his life coupled with me talking to him all the time about women. Now that he is 14, the gap for me in raising him and raising my 2 Daughters is getting wider and I don't want to mess up with him. But frankly, it is a hard job and it really does take a village

because they think they know everything. What I see often is Mothers yelling, talking down, and going off on their Sons, and that only makes our Black boys angry and bitter towards them and potentially other women. That is the look that I see in the eyes of our young men when it is done by the Mother at the school, in front of me. A look of raging bitterness. It makes me sad when I see that look in the eyes of young Black boys. So, I hope you understand that I understand the difficulty that some women are experiencing when raising Black boys. I, too, am a Black Mother and have to fight against this mindset as a Black Mother raising my Son, especially the older he gets. In actuality, I have thousands of Sons that I have helped to raise over the years. The Sons that I am talking about did not come through my womb, but through my room…my classroom that is. This, too, helps to qualify me to have this conversation with you. And let me tell you, this, is a hard conversation to have because I, too, am a Black woman, but I see so much damage being done to our Black boys that it really bothers me. I believe that we can do better if we know better.

Another reason for boys not growing up is due to high volumes of single-parent homes in our communities as well as the feminization of the males. As such, women like this subconsciously feel the need to raise their Daughters to be self-sufficient and self-preserving like them, while nurturing their Sons by shifting their desire for emotional bonding with a male. This is exactly why it can be difficult for these women to have a relationship with another man because she is giving too much power to her boy...her Son....and the man in her life cannot contend with that. Sometimes the boy's biological Father has the same issue with the Mother and the Son. This man cannot discipline the boy, so you'd better believe that if his own Father is having a hard time disciplining his own Son, any other man that comes into his life and tries to discipline him may have hell to pay. This is usually not the case when there is a strong man present and that strong man knows and understands the consequences of his Mother babying him too much. Could this also be a reason why in schools we see many young men have a problem being disciplined by men? They can take being disciplined by a woman but will rebel against a strong man. I see this all the time in the school system and it makes a lot of our men that work in the school system look like punks. If you work in an urban school system, you better come with it because many of those Black young men do not have a Black male authority figure at home and therefore, they rebel against it at school unless that male is skilled and shows that he cares in the way that young man needs to be shown. A strong man may be able to persuade the woman that he can help her with her Son IF she allows it.

I have seen single Black Mothers who have been scorned by a man subconsciously look at their Sons as being the man in her life which is why she defends him even when he is wrong. Black women have been known to go to jail for their man and will risk losing their home for their jail bound Son. Jail bound did not happen the day of the offense. Earlier in the book we saw that the boy who stole the candy out of the teacher's drawer was headed that way, remember? Don't overlook situations like that. That Black boy should be made to Never Ever want to steal again, no matter how hard it may be. I also believe that Black Mothers have to raise their Black Sons keeping in mind that they are born with two strikes against them: being born Black in America and being born a male. So, in my opinion, he has to be raised differently because the odds are stacked up against him.

I work with Mothers that I am talking about daily, and I know after reading this book, many are going to have questions for me as to what I think about their particular situation. There are Mothers that I have had personal conversations with. But many are not ready. They are in denial, and you cannot tell them otherwise. Even though I can see the problem exacerbating while they are young, Mom's usually don't identify with it as a problem until it starts impact their peace of mind, their health, their freedom, their relationships, or their job. There are women who understand their Son's behavior and what the outcome will be if she does not set boundaries. As such, it has been my experience that some Black Mothers will subconsciously safeguard their Sons from any potential harm. Consequently, this falls right in line with Black Mothers raising girls, because the Mother realizes that there is less of a chance that her Daughter will be able to depend on a Black male to provide for her, so she raises her to be a what? An Independent Black Woman! Not to depend on a man for fear that she may be done wrong by one or perhaps because she may have to pick up all the slack or maybe just because the pickings are slim. Once this cycle continues, do you know who each woman gets mad at? The man's Mother. Why? Because there are some things that only a woman can give a boy/man and if he doesn't have it, he is not going to be able to give it to his girlfriend/wife. Now the woman has an attitude toward her husband's Mother and she can't even articulate why sometimes.

Chapter Three: The 13th

The relevance of the "13th" Documentary by Ava DuVernay

Emmy Award Winning Ava DuVernay's riveting Netflix documentary, the *"13th,"* sheds light on an inhumane clause in the 13th amendment of the United States Constitution that basically legalizes slavery through criminalization. The 13th refers to the 13th Amendment that reads, *neither slavery nor involuntary servitude, except as a punishment for crime whereof the party shall have been duly convicted, shall exist within the United States, or any place subject to their jurisdiction.* Slavery technically ended over 150 years ago, and Ava DuVernay is skillful at showing us the amendment that abolished it. Narrated by various activists, lawmakers, and social influencers, the film places a particular focus on the destructive effects that the "13th Amendment" has had on the Black community as well as how U.S. corporations and multiple government administrations have been instrumental in keeping the cycle of perpetual slavery alive in Black communities for

43

decades. As an educator, I was absolutely breathless while watching this documentary, and if you have not seen it, you must see it. One of her goals for making the movie was to inspire people to "really examine their own thoughts and feelings" about how they may be complicit in the institution of mass incarceration. I was so inspired that I felt it necessary to talk about it in this book dealing with African-American Mothers and their Sons. There is so much that I did not know until I watched the documentary. My level of awareness was raised and I felt more compelled to educate and try to save our Black youth (male and female) within my sphere of influence. The "13th" is a powerful look at how the modern-day prison labor system links to slavery. The documentary inevitably shows various conversations about the criminal justice system and the fatal police shootings of African-Americans and mentions that the United States is home to five percent of the world's population, but 25 percent of the world's prisoners who are mostly Black and Hispanic. Listed below are some statistics that are given in the documentary that show the significant increase or massive expansion of the prison system which under President Clinton forced many men, like your Son, to go to prison who should not have. I took the liberty of writing down the numbers to share with you to help give you some perspective as to how you can start thinking if you have not begun already:

- 1970's U.S. Prison Population 357,292
- 1980's U.S. Prison Population 513,900
- 1985 U.S. Prison Population 759,100
- 1990 U.S. Prison Population 1,179,200
- 2000 U.S. Prison Population 2,015,300
- 2014 U.S. Prison Population 2,306,200

There is a 1 in 3 chance of your Son going to jail in his lifetime because he is a Black male. DuVernay established a connection between these alarming statistics and the post-Civil War era. The brief clause in the 13th Amendment allowed the South to rebuild its economy through prison labor and African Americans were arrested in large numbers — often for minor crimes to make sure there were laborers to get the jobs done. This reminds me of the Vagrancy Act that I remember teaching about in 5th grade Social Studies. The Vagrancy Act of 1866, passed by the General Assembly on January 15, 1866, forced into employment, for a term of up to three months, any person who appeared to be unemployed or homeless. If so-called vagrants ran away and were recaptured, they would be forced to work for no compensation while wearing balls and chains. More formally known as the Act Providing for the Punishment of Vagrants, the law came shortly after the American Civil War (1861 - 1865) when hundreds of thousands of African Americans, many of them just freed from slavery, wandered in search of work and displaced family members. In short, the system set up African-Americans because they didn't have time to find jobs right after slavery. The act criminalized free people attempting to rebuild their lives and was considered to be another form of law that would reinstitute "slavery in all but its name." The knowledge of this law sounds like much of what was presented in the 13th when describing how corporations benefit from free laborers in jail today. The thought that this became a law based on a backdoor conversation to keep Blacks in some form of slavery makes me sad. Can you imagine your Son being a part of this type of system? With statistics like every 1 - 3, maybe he already is.

Chapter Four: The Chrysalis

Your Son's Transformation Through Growth and Failure

Do you love your Son but want him to be more responsible? Are you an African-American Mother that feels that you did everything you could for your Son and expected or are expecting him to grow into a happy, healthy, and successful young man that makes good decisions? But he hasn't, at least not yet, and you keep asking yourself when will you get a breakthrough? It is quite possible that your desire to see your Son succeed may have left little room for him to make his own mistakes and learn from them. Could it be that you commanded your Son's development by over-parenting and being overprotective of him? Could you be a "Helicopter Mom" even though your Son is 10, 20, 30, 40 or 50 years old? Helicoptering is an epidemic that you probably started when your Son was very young. Instilling a fear of failure occurs when parents step in all areas at all ages from toddlerhood throughout high school and adulthood. Helicopter Moms like you tend to insert themselves into activities best left for children to figure out for themselves. Too many Mothers yell instructions from the sidelines at sporting events, help too much with homework and will lie and say their Son did it but the child can barely do the work at school. Perfectly done homework, riiiight, and will question teachers about grades in front of the child, as well as interfere too much in their children's problems. Is this you? A helicopter Mom removes her Son's decision-making powers and the ability to learn how to bounce back after making a mistake. Failure is an outcome that most of us dread but must deal with. Example, one day a client called me because her level of awareness had been raised through my coaching techniques and she did not want to make a bad decision and stunt his or her growth again. She called because her Son wanted money from her again and she did not want to give it to him but she had trouble saying no to him. Of course, he gave her his sob story about what he didn't have and nobody ever helps him (violin plays) and she was about to give it to him because it would help him with bus fare to help him find a job. In my conversation with her, I summarized the story relating her

Son's struggle to that of the butterfly. I told her that if she helped him by giving him the money, he may die or become crippled. She was a little frustrated and wanted to trust me on this but she also knew she needed my perspective to help her to "see clearly." Read below and make the analogy yourself.

The Caterpillar Stage

In this stage of the butterfly's life (which follows right after hatching from an egg) the main task is consumption. The caterpillar's purpose is simply to eat as much as possible in order to fuel the growth that will take place in the future. During this stage, the caterpillar will outgrow and shed its skin as many as four or five times.

The Chrysalis Stage

This is the most intriguing stage of butterfly development, which appears catastrophic from the perspective of the caterpillar. When the little crawler is fully grown and can eat no more, it simply dangles from a branch and spins a protective cocoon around itself so it can safely rest and digest all the food that has been consumed in the previous stage. Though the chrysalis (your Son) appears unchanged from the outside during this stage, there is dramatic transformation taking place inside of him: the body of the caterpillar is slowly dissolving while the previously dormant precursor cells of the emerging butterfly ("imaginal cells") gradually develop, migrate together and *create a brand new being*.

The Butterfly Stage

At last in this final stage, the fully developed butterfly is ready to emerge from the chrysalis. After breaking free, the butterfly's wings are still folded and wet and more rest time is necessary to allow blood to flow into the wings. Finally, when the unfurled wings are fully dry, the butterfly is ready to take flight and share its beauty with the world.

It Is Ok for Your Son to Struggle (story)

Once a little boy was playing outdoors and found a fascinating caterpillar. He carefully picked it up and took it home to show his Mother. He asked his Mother if he could keep it, and she said he could if he would take good care of it.

The little boy got a large jar from his Mother and put plants to eat, and a stick to climb on, in the jar. Every day he watched the caterpillar and brought it new plants to eat. One day the caterpillar climbed up the stick and started acting strangely. The boy worriedly called his Mother who came and understood that the caterpillar was creating a cocoon. The Mother explained to the boy how the caterpillar was going to go through a metamorphosis and become a butterfly.

The little boy was thrilled to hear about the changes his caterpillar would go through. He watched every day, waiting for the butterfly to emerge. One day it happened, a small hole appeared in the cocoon and the butterfly started to struggle to come out.

At first the boy was excited, but soon he became concerned. The butterfly was struggling so hard to get out! It looked like it couldn't break free! It looked desperate! It looked like it was making no progress!

The boy was so concerned he decided to help. He ran to get scissors, and then walked back. He thought he would help the chrysalis by snipping the cocoon to make the hole bigger so the butterfly could escape!

As the butterfly came out, the boy was surprised. It had a swollen body and small, shriveled wings. He continued to watch the butterfly expecting that, at any moment, the wings would dry out, enlarge and expand to support the swollen body. He knew that in time the body would shrink and the butterfly's wings would expand like they were supposed to. But neither happened! The butterfly spent the rest of its life crawling around with a swollen body and shriveled wings. It never was able to fly...

As the boy tried to figure out what had gone wrong, his Mother took him to talk to a scientist from a local college. He learned that the butterfly was SUPPOSED to struggle. Your Son is SUPPOSED to struggle. How is he going to lead a family...call you?

In fact, the butterfly's struggle to push its way through the tiny opening of the cocoon is what pushes the fluid out of its body and into its wings. WITHOUT THE STRUGGLE, the butterfly would never, ever fly. The boy's good intentions hurt the butterfly just like your good intentions are hurting your Son.

Name: _Mom_

Date: TODAY

R~x~

Dosage: Please take the following prescription for the rest of your life at least 3-4 times throughout the day for a restful night's sleep and in order to get your life back.

Side Effects for Not Taking as Prescribed: Sadness, heartache, heart palpitations, busted eye vessels due to stress, worry, anxiety, sleepless nights, crazy making, broken heart, death.

Take Prescription as Follows:
1. Admit there is a problem
2. Say No
3. Change Your Thinking
4. Stop Making Excuses
5. Be Able to Identify When You Are Being Manipulated
6. Invest in Yourself
7. Get a Life
8. Celebrate Every Small Victory

Doctor's Signature: Dr. Leslie

Chapter Five: 8 Practical Solutions

Step 1: Admit there is a Problem

You can begin to solve your problem when you admit you have one. This is not about your Son right now, this is about you.

Assignment: After taking into consideration everything that you have read in this book, what have you decided is the problem and what are you going to do about it? Use a journal to complete your weekly assignments. Think about when your Son was younger how you may have enabled him in various situations. Think and journal why you believe you did it? Was there an incident in his life that you felt guilty about and you somehow overcompensated? Write about it. Don't stop writing or crying until you feel empty. This exercise is to build your reality check muscle so that you can get real with yourself so that you can get on the road to getting your peace and your joy back. Use as many pages as you need to in your journal to write as much as you want. Dump it all out. Relax and Release! You may have to do it again later, so write in a separate journal, and keep the journal safe.

Step 2: Learn to Say No

It is not heartless to say no. You can do it. If whenever you say no to your Son you feel heartless, inadequate, un-loving, or like you will do anything to keep the peace out of obligation of being his Mother, then it is time to change how you think. Your change begins with you as you start putting up boundaries then calmly continue making sure your set boundaries are respected. Only you can do this. Change happens as you challenge those disruptive, deep, subconscious beliefs that are wreaking havoc on your decision making process, and you may not even be aware that they are there. These deep subconscious beliefs are feeding your conscious beliefs. Your conscious beliefs are feeding your self-talk; the things you say to yourself, your internal conversation whether positive or negative. Through Group or One on One Coaching, I help you with positive self-talk in a structured way by attending 8 weekly sessions online, one weekly call where information is provided in order to get transformation, and a group call is held where you are on a call with other Mothers who are going through the same thing and you have an opportunity to ask questions. This gives you the opportunity to learn from others and know that you are not alone. Positive self-talk training helps you become aware of inaccurate or negative thinking so you can view challenging situations more clearly and respond to them in a more effective way. This can be an effective tool to help you learn how to better manage stressful life situations and will help you face and deal with a wide range of issues such as identifying ways to manage your emotions, resolving relationship conflicts and learning better ways to communicate with your Son.

Engaging in this deliberate self-talk is a way of exploring painful feelings, emotions and experiences, therefore, you may feel emotionally uncomfortable at times. You may cry, get upset or feel angry during a challenging session, or you may also feel physically drained. The good thing is that if you react this way during a group session, other people will have received help by listening and watching your responses as well, and you will feel like something in your life is happening and know that it is ok.

Not if, but when this challenging situation occurs with your Son, you will have to hold onto the simple, yet powerful and accurate things that you say to yourself to create new pathways in your brain in order to reprogram your way of thinking. When those challenging situations occur, you have to hold onto your new way of thinking like a drowning person holding onto a life jacket. But you have to have your new mindset in place before anything jumps off. For example, your Son calls you because he ran out of gas for the 4th time, and he wants you to come and bring the gas can and purchase the gas. You are already tired of going to rescue him whenever he runs out of gas. It has become when, not if, he runs out of gas. You start thinking to yourself, *why does he always call me when he runs out of gas?* Other people tell him they can't help him, so when he calls you, he gives you the sob story that nobody will help him and he doesn't have any money to get gas and he is way out in the middle of nowhere and he hopes that nobody comes to kill him since he is Black...etc. You know the rest of the story. So Mom, you have to shift your mindset before the call comes...before the phone rings. That is how you get your strength to say no. You may feel like a horrible Mom for not helping your Son during "his time of need" but if you already know that you don't know if you can say no to your Son while practicing self talk, then you definitely will not say no when he calls. As you regain your power through your newfound assertiveness, you will be able to stick to the boundaries that you set. Now when your Son comes to you with another request that you don't feel good about doing, you already know to have your positive self-talk playing in your head and hold on to your life jacket so that you don't drown. In the same way that you can't learn to swim while you are drowning, you must learn the techniques of swimming before drowning, likewise, you cannot learn to change your thinking in the middle of an emotional situation with your Son that you want to avoid.

Mom, you are a rescuer by nature and you tend to get your self-worth or value from feeling needed or being approved. Please know that there is a tendency for guilt to manifest inside of you when you start shifting your mindset and building boundaries with your positive self talk in preparation to say no. You will feel guilty! You will feel like a bad Mother. You will feel like you should help your Son since you are his Mother. You will also feel like he should be able to call on *you*, if no one else, since you are his Mother.

That feeling of being a bad Mother is lying to you, and as hard as it may be, you need to shift your mindset. Go into your subconscious mind and practice your new self-talk to hear and listen to the boundaries that you took the time to create. If you respond to your Son like you normally would, then you are rescuing him from his consequences. This is how I got the title of one of my other books, *Rescue My Son From M*e. It means that Mother keeps enabling her Son and she now knows that she is not doing him any good, but she loves him so much that she can't Rescue her Son from herself, she needs someone's help to save her Son from HER! The Son needs to be rescued from Mom because if he knew the boundaries, he would follow the boundaries. He needs to be rescued from (you) because (you) keep rescuing him from all of his problems thus making them yours, and you wonder why you are stressed out. Don't be wishy-washy. Try your best not to let your Son push you into changing your mind. Learn to say "no" with some strength behind it when you mean it. If too often your "no" becomes a "yes" because your Son has been successful at wearing you down, a pattern of emotional blackmail can result. Your Son has learned that being relentless works; if his relentlessness still hasn't gotten him what he wants, in his mind it means that he should be even more relentless until he's successful. He won't see anything wrong with his behavior either because it's what he's used to doing. The greatest danger is that he'll be in charge instead of you. So say "no," state your reason, make it short and to the point, and walk away. This takes practice but commit in your mind to doing it as many times as it takes until it becomes a part of you.

Disengaging from the discussion. If your Son is asking you for something you have some flexibility on, you might listen to his argument as long as he's respectful. If it seems reasonable to you, you might decide to change your "no" to a "yes." However, if you don't change your mind, only discuss it with him to a certain point. Stop giving him your counterpoints and disengage. You'll know when it's time for you to stop when you feel the early signs of your adrenaline rising—your heart will beat faster, your face may get hot, and you might start to feel shaky. Pay attention to this and swiftly end the conversation and disengage. And how do you disengage when your child does not? Don't say another word. Walk into another room or out of the house if your Son is old enough; ride it out. Engaging at all, in any way, will only add fuel to the fire. Holding onto yourself with your *no*, despite what your Son does communicates that *No matter what you do, I will not lose myself. No matter how long you carry on, I will not give in. I will not allow your behavior to affect me.*

Assignment: This week, use your journal to write down your self-talk this week whether it is positive or negative. What lies are you telling yourself? What lies are you listening to? How did you respond to your Son this week?

Did you have any success saying no to him or did you come close to saying no but caved in? How did you feel about yourself in the midst of the situation? What did you realize about yourself? Is this something that you feel that you can do or do you feel that you are too weak and vulnerable where your Son is concerned?

Step 3: Positive Self-Talk - Daily Affirmation

Let's face it, you are an African-American Mother that did everything you could for your Son and with all of his talents, skills, and abilities, you expected him to grow into a happy, healthy, and successful young man in the community. But he hasn't, at least, not yet—and even though the problems that you continue to rescue him from didn't just start yesterday, you are fully aware that his problems threaten your peace of mind, your health, your freedom, your relationship with your husband/boyfriend, your job or other family relationships and it has to stop. Now! This week we are going to talk about self-talk, rewards and consequences. At the end of the chapter, you will find a positive self talk affirmation that you need to memorize or select the verses that pertain to you and say them several times each day to build up your self confidence as you practice saying no to your Son. You may find that your confidence will build up and spill over into other areas of your life where you have had challenges asserting yourself. After you read this chapter, you will find the positive self-talk and daily affirmation at the end of the chapter. Make copies or keep this book with you with the positive self-talk pages marked.

Positive Affirmation

Is your glass half-empty or half-full? How you answer this question about positive thinking may reflect your outlook on life, your attitude toward yourself, and whether you're optimistic or pessimistic — and it may even affect your health.

Indeed, some studies show that personality traits such as optimism and pessimism can affect many areas of your health and well-being. The positive thinking that usually comes with optimism is a key part of effective stress management. And effective stress management is associated with many health benefits. If you tend to be pessimistic, you can learn positive thinking skills.

Understanding positive thinking and self-talk

Positive thinking helps you approach unpleasant things and situations in a more positive and productive way. You think the best is going to happen, not the worst.

Positive thinking often starts with self-talk. Self-talk is the endless stream of unspoken thoughts that run through your head. These automatic thoughts can be positive or negative. Some of your self-talk comes from logic and reason. Other self-talk may arise from misconceptions that you create because of lack of information. If the thoughts that run through your head are mostly negative, your outlook on life is more likely pessimistic. If your thoughts are mostly positive, you're likely an optimist — someone who practices positive thinking.

The health benefits of positive thinking

Let's face it, worrying about your Son and trying to meet his demands are compromising your health. Researchers continue to explore the effects of positive thinking and optimism on health. Health benefits that positive thinking may provide include:

- Increased life span
- Lower rates of depression
- Lower levels of distress
- Greater resistance to the common cold
- Better psychological and physical well-being
- Better cardiovascular health and reduced risk of death from cardiovascular disease
- Better coping skills during hardships and times of stress

Having a positive outlook enables you to cope better with stressful situations, which reduces the harmful health effects of stress on your body.

It's also thought that positive and optimistic people tend to live healthier lifestyles — they get more physical activity, follow a healthier diet, and don't smoke or drink alcohol in excess.

Identifying negative thinking

Not sure if your self-talk is positive or negative? Some common forms of negative self-talk include:

- **Filtering.** You magnify the negative aspects of a situation and filter out all of the positive ones. For example, you had a great day at work. You completed your tasks ahead of time and were complimented for doing a speedy and thorough job. That evening, you focus only on your plan to do even more tasks and forget about the compliments you received.

- **Personalizing.** When something bad occurs with your Son, you automatically blame yourself. For example, he cancels from coming to an evening out with the family and you tell yourself the change in plans is because he did not want to be around you.

- **Catastrophizing.** You automatically anticipate the worst. The drive-through coffee shop gets your order wrong and you automatically tell

yourself that the rest of your day will be a
disaster.

- **Polarizing.** You see things only as either good
  or bad. There is no middle ground. You feel that
  you have to be perfect or you're a total failure.

Focusing on positive thinking

You can learn to turn negative thinking into positive
thinking. The process is simple, but it does take time and
practice — you're creating a new habit, after all. Here are
some ways to think and behave in a more positive and
optimistic way:

- **Identify areas to change.** If you want to
  become more optimistic, first identify areas of
  your life that you usually think negatively about,
  whether it's work, your daily commute or
  relationship with your Son. You can start small
  by focusing on one area to approach in a more
  positive way.

- **Check yourself.** Periodically during the day,
  stop and evaluate what you're thinking. If you

find that your thoughts are mainly negative, try to find a way to put a positive spin on them.

- **Be open to humor.** Give yourself permission to smile or laugh, especially during difficult times. Seek humor in everyday happenings. When you can laugh at life, you feel less stressed.
- **Follow a healthy lifestyle.** Aim to exercise for about 30 minutes on most days of the week. You can also break it up into 10-minute chunks of time during the day. Exercise can positively affect mood and reduce stress. Follow a healthy diet to fuel your mind and body. And learn techniques to manage stress.
- **Surround yourself with positive people.** Make sure those in your life are positive, supportive people you can depend on to give helpful advice and feedback. Negative people may increase your stress level and make you doubt your ability to manage stress in healthy ways.
- **Practice positive self-talk.** Start by following one simple rule: Don't say anything to yourself

that you wouldn't say to anyone else. Be gentle and encouraging with yourself. If a negative thought enters your mind, evaluate it rationally and respond with affirmations of what is good about you. Think about things you're thankful for in your life. Practice gratitude.

Your new positive self-talk affirmation. Learn this and practice daily. In your journal, write what parts of the affirmation mean the most to you right now and why. Take those parts and commit them to memory and just say those phrases until they become a part of you.

I am a great Mother, and I am not being cruel when I say no to my Son. I am not depriving him of anything; at least not anything that he really needs. Their reaction and mood is their responsibility, not mine.

Just because I am feeling guilty doesn't make me bad. It just means I have a conscious. It is an old feeling that used to manipulate me. My new boundaries are healthy and I am proud of my new boundaries. It makes me feel good about myself.

My feelings are not in charge of me anymore.

My feelings can be wrong - if they are misrepresenting my reality, then I know it is ok to talk back to them. My emotions in this situation are lying to me, they are reflecting my past beliefs and conclusions that were wrong. But NO MORE!

My Son's overreaction or rejection to my new boundaries say more about him than it says about me. Enabling my Son will not buy me love. I have to take care of myself. By setting healthy boundaries between me and my Son, I am protecting my empathy and stopping myself from being resentful towards my Son which is why I am making sure I can continue to be a helpful, loving person. If my self-worth or value lies in the hands of my Son, then I risk him taking it away from me at any time. If I only focus on feeling guilty about giving my Son what he wants, then there is no room in my life for positive change.

Mom, say this daily, study this daily, believe this daily, practice this daily. You are worth it!

Step 4: Stop Making Excuses for Your Son

It doesn't matter how old your Son is, you have to stop making excuses for him. Our Sons know what they want, but they don't always know what they need. When Sons are spoiled or never given the opportunity to work through struggles, they won't be given one of the most important skills in adulthood–the ability to self-regulate. You know those adults: They are the ones who expect the world to revolve around them, come to work when they feel like it, explode over minute things, and never seem happy. In order to have Sons who are content, work hard and respect authority, the expectations need to be set in childhood. If this is what you want for your Son, then consider the following:

Common excuses include: *He did not get enough sleep. He is bored. He is gifted. He needs to be challenged more. Boys will be boys. I do not know why he does that. Your child is bothering my Son, He has ADD. He has ADHD.* Your excuses have only enabled your Son to repeat bad behavior without consequences or without the correct consequences or without consistent consequences. Meaning, you said one thing but did not stick to it. Children usually exhibit bad behavior at an early age. Parents, too tired to correct the bad behavior, allow it to continue. Permissive parents *give in.* Many Mothers fear that the consequences for bad behavior are too strict - not loving. Without correction, the child continues the bad behavior. Most parents are embarrassed when their child misbehaves. Looks from other parents suggest that they are to blame. Some parents do blame themselves. They know they have allowed their child to continue to use bad behavior. Excuses make some parents feel better. Parents who make excuses for their Son's bad behavior are teaching their Son to use those same excuses in other areas of his life. As a result, your Son continues exhibiting bad behavior, and you accept it. However, people like me do not accept it. Sooner or later, the child suffers hurt, regret and loneliness. Are you the Mom who makes excuses every time your Son acts up? If so – stop it. Expect him to behave in a positive manner and state what you expect. Excuses for your adult Son sound more like this:

I'm just helping him get through the week until he gets a new job.

He is just taking a break before he looks for job.

He doesn't know how to cook so I have to cook for him.

He is not an addict. He just drinks a few beers when he is depressed.

I know he wrecked 3 cars already, but perhaps if I give him back his car he can find a job and can get to work.

I know he is not working but at least he is not in jail.

Yes, he is a grown man that plays video games all day, but at least I know where he is.

He is not an alcoholic. He is just a social drinker.

I don't want anything to happen to him. I don't want him to die!

Do any of these excuses sound remotely familiar? No matter how old your Son is 20 or 50, the Ideal Reader for this book has made plenty of excuses for her Son. Have you? For your next journal assignment, (Day 1) ask yourself the following questions. What role have you played in making excuses for your Son? What is the worst excuse that you can remember that you made for your Son, meaning, you knew it was an excuse, but you wanted to cover for him because either you didn't want to look bad or you did not want him to look bad? What excuses are you making for him right now? How have you hurt your Son by making excuses for him? What relationships have you damaged by taking up for your Son and making excuses for him?

(Day 1) Take a day and just reflect on the above questions.

(Day 2) Take out your journal and begin to go deep within yourself to answer the questions. If you want to ask someone a question to help validate one of your answers, you can, just be honest with yourself. Completion of this step is to help get you one step closer to your peace, your joy, and being able to move on with your life.

(Day 3) After 24 hours have passed, I want you to read your responses. Decide if you still agree with your responses. Feel free to add to those responses if you think about anything else. After reading your responses, write down how you feel about yourself. Write down how you feel about your Son. When you think about the excuses that you have made for your Son in the past, which one do you feel did the most damage to his current life? If you could change the excuses that you made for your Son, what would you change or do over today?

(Day 4) Write a letter to your Son, but you are not going to give it to him. Put it in a sealed envelope and tuck it away so that only you can find it. You will need it at a later date.

(Day 5) Go back and reread the questions above. If you are truly ready to help your Son, ask someone close to you how they feel you have hurt your Son, and be prepared to receive the answer, in love, even if they are not very nice about it but you know they are truthful. Journal their responses. How did you feel about the person's answers? Did you agree or disagree? What did you disagree with and why? Were you hurt by their response? Do you believe they have your best interest at heart? Now, what are you going to do with this information? Make sure you put a date on all of your journal pages.

Step 5: Identify When You Are Being Manipulated By Your Son

Does your Son use anger or threats to get what he wants from you? Does he pick fights and blackmail you emotionally? Or maybe he acts helpless or plays sick to get out of doing things that he should be responsible enough to handle but you end up doing them. Whether your Son manipulates you aggressively or passively, his behavior makes you feel out of control and "played" by him. I believe many, if not most parents have felt manipulated by their child at one time or another. Teens in particular can be very adept at manipulative behaviors that run the gamut from flattery and charm to downright abuse to get what they want. And most kids, by the time they get to adolescence, are skilled at arguing, debating and raging to get their way. That is why it is extremely important to nip this type of behavior in the bud when your Son is very young. No means no, but in most of their minds, *no* means *yes*. Mom just needs more clarification to understand the matter and then she will say yes. At least that is what your Son thinks. You might be sitting there saying to yourself, *I would never have spoken to my parents the way my Son talks to me.* Back in the day, most parents valued obedience and used hitting, withdrawal of love and fear to scare kids into submission, and it worked. You have to do what works for you so that you can get your peace and joy back. You will not get it back continuing to allow your Son to manipulate you. So, you have some major decisions to make. Let me ask you this, do you know that you are being manipulated by your Son? Write your answer in your journal. Are you ready to stop being manipulated by him? Write your response in your journal. On a scale of 1 - 10, how ready are you to stop being manipulated by your Son? What areas can you identify that your Son manipulates you often? When you see him coming or when you see a certain sweet behavior, you may know within your inner core that he is about to ask you for some money. Perhaps if he is gone for too long, you start getting a little paranoid because you start feeling like he is going to call you with some type of emergency that is going to disrupt the flow of your day. You have to first decide that you have been manipulated constantly by your Son and also decide that you are not going to allow him to do it to you anymore. You are going to have to read chapter 3 again and get some more ideas on how to change your thinking so that when you feel you are being manipulated the next time, you will be ready. Just remember, you are disrupting their natural behavior of manipulation that they have been doing for a while, so don't think manipulative behavior is going to stop just because you want it to. Has your Son ever made you feel like you are crazy? This can happen with our older and younger Sons. There is a term actually called Crazy making. Crazy making throws you off-balance mentally or emotionally making you easier to control. Abusers carry out crazy making in many ways. Oh, you never thought of your Son's behavior towards you as abuse? Think again. It can be considered emotional abuse which is why I encourage you to do more research into that specific topic. Usually crazy making is done so often and so easily for your Son that you don't even know he is doing it. For example, your Son may say one thing and then swear they said the opposite or didn't say it at all and claim that you are crazy, unbalanced, forgetful, and out to get them when you are not even thinking like that.

If you're a victim of crazy making, you often feel lost, disconnected, and unsure of yourself. You learn to doubt your perceptions because every time you say *The sky is blue* your Son says, *The sky is green*. Over time, you become brainwashed enough to accept that the sky is green and perhaps you were wrong...again! Crazy making makes you feel like you are the crazy one. But you can stop this cycle, one day at time, if you are ready. Your Son is relying on you being in the dark about what they're doing to you. So, if you can recognize this behavior as it's happening to you, you can continue to educate yourself so that you are empowered to do something about it and not be abused. I know it is hurtful at first when you first come to really know that you are being manipulated by your own Son. But the sooner you come to grips with it, the sooner you will get your joy back. You're a survivor.

No means No.

It can be a lot of pressure on you to be very intentional about showing your Son how to be a man of integrity. Do this by first exhibiting those qualities within yourself. That means that when you say NO, you should mean NO even though that is not what he may want to hear or if his feelings get hurt in the process. Your own feelings may even get hurt when you say no because you really want to say yes, but you know that saying yes right now would not be beneficial for your Son in the long-run. When you say No when you mean No, you are helping your Son to become a man. When you don't stick to your word, you are subconsciously demonstrating to your Son that he doesn't need to stick to his word either. You will develop your inner strength the more you make or allow yourself to say no to your Son. Crazy making or not, you might have to show him crazy to get your point across. When you say what you mean and mean what you say, your Son may not like your new assertiveness but he will respect your word and know that when you say something, you mean it. This will help him grow into a man that knows how to respect other people's decisions as well.

Assignment: Continue to write in your journal answering the following questions: What resonated most for you in this chapter? Did you identify with any of the crazy making behavior? If so, then how? Give some examples. Do you know anyone else close to you that exhibits crazy making behavior such as a Father, Mother, Spouse, or Friend? If so, describe their behavior and how it makes you feel when you see it. What are your takeaways from this chapter? What do you know without a shadow of a doubt that you are going to do to stop allowing yourself to be abused by your Son? Does the word abuse even resonate with you? How did you feel when you read about the possibility of you being emotionally abused? Write about your new self. How do you see yourself responding to manipulation and crazy making behavior from your Son?

Step 6: Take Time to Care for Yourself

Many women lose their own identity once they become a
Mother. While in pursuit of being a good Mother you
forgot to be kind to the most important person, you. As you
train yourself and sometimes force or commit to yourself
that you will take care of our own needs first, you have to
forgive yourself first for taking care of everyone else first
and not yourself. You have to forgive yourself to talk
yourself into believing that you are right. You have to
engage in self-talk so that you are not filled with guilt as a
result of doing something for yourself. As Mothers, we
tend to believe that we should give our children everything
many times not leaving any money, time, peace, food, or
energy for ourselves. There is a fine line between not
giving them everything and taking care of yourself.

The best gift that you can give your Son, and more
importantly, your family, is a Mother that is whole. You
need to like yourself, you should know yourself and respect
yourself enough to create your own life experiences so that
you can make good sound decisions. Making this decision

first will give you a peace of mind later. This can mean that there are times that you only take time for you, and this is difficult for a lot of Mothers who spend their time putting out fires and meeting the needs of their Sons.

I remember when my children were younger, I liked to eat at Zaxby's every once in a while, but never with my children around. When I wanted some time for myself, I would go to Zaxby's and sit in the parking lot eating my salad in the car by myself. That salad tasted so good. The best part of it all is I did not have to share it with anyone. Nobody asked me for any of it because it was only me, myself, and I throwing down on that Zaxby's Zalad. I saw a commercial one day that depicted this very scenario. I started laughing so hard because I knew exactly how that lady was feeling.

When we think about identity theft, we think about an impostor posing as another person. Yet in Motherhood, we are the imposters in our own lives. And it is the result of the admirable quality of wanting to give everything to our Son and leaving nothing for yourself. We forget the most important rule of self preservation: you cannot give *long-term* what you do not have. Also, you can share more of who you are with your children as you connect with the woman you once were. Making the decision to end the *Silent War* within yourself is the decision that each of us has to make in our own time and season.

You have a say in what happens in your own life. You are the Captain of your ship. You have the pen. You write the script. Stop letting your Son write YOUR script AND HIS. So, in order for you, Mom, to get control of your life, you need to come to grips with where you are in your life and in the life of your Son. Begin to truly love you and your Son enough to let him go and grow up. Letting him go and grow up may mean not responding to every little thing that he does or says. Stop being helicopter Mom. Stop running to the school everytime he says somebody did or said something to him that he wants you to show up and do something about. I knew a lady who had 5 grown boys whose marriages were destroyed because she was in control and their wives could not tolerate her controlling their marriages through her Sons. The oldest Son was 50 at the time and his Mother would call his job and talk to his boss and tell his boss that he couldn't come into work because he was sick. She did it every single time. Do you think his wife respected him? She was married to a grown boy. I can see that now. Mom did not have a life of her own. Her life consisted of controlling the lives of her Sons even as married adults. You have to stop being your Son's Superwoman. Stop listening to all of his excuses and stop making excuses for his excuses, invest in yourself and get a life of your own.

Assignment

Here are **5 Ways to Reconnect with Who You Are after making the decision to put yourself first.**

1. Create a weekly schedule that allows you some time alone. Select the same day and time of the week and schedule this time on an ongoing basis and don't let someone else's emergency pull you away from doing it.

2. Ask yourself, "What can I do right now to make me happier?" Whether it's being happier at home, at work, finding a new hobby or volunteering, your next step is to act on what you have realized.

3. Create a vision board of simple goals that you have for your life. Include your plans like graduate school, starting your business, losing 50 lbs from the baby weight that came on 1 year ago or 20 years ago. You can complete a 5k or join a gym, for example.

4. Be intentional about doing something that you enjoy doing or perhaps something that you once enjoyed but stopped doing. Riding a bike, yoga, calling and talking to old friends, going to the movies.

5. Join Social Media communities to connect with other women that you can relate with and that might have non-judgmental solutions to help you in your journey.

In addition to completing the above assignments, what did you do this week to intentionally take care of yourself. Describe your experience in detail. How do you feel? What did you do? Did you feel guilty or empowered? Write out and explain all of your thoughts.

Step 7: Get a Life

Your adult children, whether they are living with you or whether they are constantly keeping you at their beck and call, need to come to terms with the fact that you now have a separate life from them. Unless it is your aim in life to be with your Son as long as he needs you, then you need to help him understand that you do not belong to him. You are not his maid, you are not his personal bank where he makes withdrawals whenever he needs them, but never makes deposits. You are not his fixer that whenever something goes wrong in his life, its Mom TO THE RESCUE! It is important that you have a conversation with your Son and let him know that you are working to rebuild your life. Let him know that you have begun to engage in some new adventures in life and will not be as readily available to him as you have been in the past. He is not going to believe you, yet. You can also demonstrate that you *are separating your life from his by getting your own life* through your actions *and not words.* Actions speak louder than words. For example, for those of you who have grandchildren and love to be with them, you still have to build your own life apart from theirs. Your Son calls you and casually tells you that he needs you to watch his children tonight while he goes to work. My thoughts would be, *did you have a babysitter before? Why are you calling me now?* Now, you may feel guilty about saying no because you are accustomed to saying ok, and perhaps you really want to watch your grandchildren, but with your new mindset, you watch his children on your terms not because it became an emergency situation. If you have other plans, do not cancel them. Now is the time for your Son to respect the fact that you have plans of your own and are separate from his and you need privacy and space. It is up to you to help them understand that you will help them when you can or if you decide you want to help, but the choice is yours. These are your terms, these are your boundaries. Remember in this case, your Son is old enough to lead his own life. This change in behavior on your part with consistency and sticking to your plan, will force and/or encourage your Son to respect your time as well as the other things you are doing in your life. When your Son calls you out of the blue and expects you to help him out or meet his need, it is the same behavior that he has demonstrated and expected of you for years. How dare you try to take away his apple cart. As a matter of fact, he is not going to really believe that you are serious until you show him that you are serious about moving on with your life. He is not going to expect you to say no. He is not going to expect you to put yourself before him, so the problems and requests that he calls you for will get worse and worse before getting better because he subconsciously wants to prove to you that you can't break away from him because he needs you and he is still in control.

Assignment: In your journal, write how you plan to get a life. What does your new life consist of? What new things do you engage in? How will you separate yourself from your Son while still loving him and moving on with your life? How will you prepare for the resistance that you will encounter with your Son once you try to get a life?

Step 8: Celebrate Every Small Victory!

In your day to day life, you will normally perform some activity which qualifies as a *win or victory*. It could be as small as remembering to eat healthy or not respond to your Son's demands as you normally would have. That is huge and you need to celebrate yourself and recognize it as a win. Small victories will go unnoticed unless you tell yourself that you are going to celebrate yourself. While it is important to notice your mistakes so that you can correct them, you should not ignore your small wins. This is because they give you joy and are essential to your motivation. Here is how to celebrate small wins daily and increase your happiness so that you can get control of your life and get your peace back.

Notice Your Small Wins

What exactly is a small win? This is a behavior which you now do successfully, but used to struggle with it and weren't sure you could actually pull off. A small win varies from Mother to Mother. It can be not giving into your Son's manipulation to taking the time to grow a flower or sticking to a workout plan. Small wins do not change the world. However, they can put a smile on your face and help you gain some self-confidence. We can get stuck on noticing all the bad activities going on in our lives and forget to see the small wins. Small wins give us the strength to reach further and try to accomplish more. Hence, they are essential in the process of growth. Take the time to notice your small wins so as to appreciate them and yourself, too.

Get Excited!

Children get very excited about small things. This keeps them happy and enthusiastic about life. As we grow up, we become dull and uninspired due to life's challenges. It becomes difficult to get excited about things that do not qualify as big and significant. Don't subconsciously fail to get excited by small things in a bid to impress other adults. The questions is, why would you limit your happiness to impress other people who simply don't care and are just as grumpy or negative as you may be? If you get excited about small things, let it show. If you feel happy because you were finally able to do that small thing that you have struggled with for a long time, then get excited about it. Let it be your small win. Bask in the victory of having achieved it and it will increase your level of happiness.

Communicate your small wins

Human beings are social beings. We communicate with each other so as to share ideas or moments. Therefore, if you experience a small victory, you should tell someone who cares about it. Find a way to verbalize your small win and tell it to someone else. This will create a little celebration party for you and your friend. Doing this will make you want to experience the party again and motivate you to keep making small victories. On the other hand, it could actually motivate your friend to try out the activity that you did successfully. Everybody wins.

Establish habits which help you to make small wins every day

For you to have something to celebrate, it is important to actually make an effort to win. To make progress on a daily basis, you need to learn how to win consistently. This can only be accomplished by forming habits. These are activities which you perform without thinking about it. They come naturally to you because you have programmed your mind and body to suit them. Therefore, strive to create habits that ensure daily wins. How can you do this? Simply create and follow a plan that helps you to win more and more every day such as some of the activities mentioned in Step 7. Establish them in the fields of life that you enjoy. To create a winning habit, perform a constructive activity every day for 21 days consecutively. This will help you to experience small wins every day and increases your happiness.

Live in the present moment and acknowledge it

In pursuit of future achievements, we tend to take the present moment for granted. We think that the little activities that we perform presently do not affect us and our trajectory. As a matter of fact, they do. Day to day moments are the ones which add up and help us to have a life experience. By noticing and filling them with wins, we can create a big success eventually. For example, you strive to read 5 pages of a book every day or take the time to walk in the mornings whereas before, you would not have taken the time for yourself to do this. CELEBRATE GOOD TIMES, COME ON! Therefore, live in the present and fill it with wins. They will add up and make you a happier person, but you are creating your best self. You are being intentional about the direction of your life by celebrating yourself for every little thing.

Reward yourself

A reward is anything that brings you pleasure. You should always reward yourself for achieving anything. It could be a big or a small win. Take the time to reward yourself. This can be your favorite dish, some time watching your favorite show, something sweet. Celebrate your small wins with a reward. This motivates you to maintain focus and to program yourself for long term achievement and happiness whatever that means to you.

Don't Put Pressure On Yourself

Remember that as you celebrate your small wins, there are some areas that may take you a little longer to start winning at. Go easy on yourself right here. Pick yourself up and start over the next second. Perhaps you gave in to giving your Son some money and you really did not want to and you felt defeated afterwards. Well you know he is coming back, so you will have another opportunity to make a better decision; one that you will feel good about and can celebrate yourself. This helps you to accomplish small wins every day and leads to happiness. It also motivates you. It is important to stay motivated in life. You can do this by celebrating small wins. The guidelines above are essential tips on how to do this. Learn how to celebrate the small wins so that you can reach the big ones and appreciate yourself more.

Conclusion

Mom, you may have to read this book or certain chapters that appealed to you over and over again. Use the insights to retrain your thinking and your self-talk. Repeatedly read Chapter 3, Change Your Thinking, to help you create new ways of thinking and to set new boundaries for yourself. Use your new perspective to communicate your new way of thinking with dignified assertiveness. Remember that you are a loving, empathetic and helpful person by nature. By doing what you say you are going to do and enforcing it, you are actually loving yourself and loving your Son in one of the best ways possible. Remember the caterpillar and butterfly analogy. It is ok for your Son to struggle. The struggle is where he will get his strength and grow into a better man. I hope this book makes you feel in control of your life as you challenge your new belief system every step of the way. It doesn't stop here. Your new mindset shift will take time, consistency and structure. Celebrate small wins and go easy on yourself when you feel defeated. The journey is just as important as the destination. Family and friends can be an excellent support system. If it is possible, allow them to be a part of your world. You have to be free from the guilt and potentially the pride that plagues you and makes you suffer in silence. Finally, put your Son in God's hands. God has lended him to you while he is on this earth. He is God's child first. Love your Son and be there for him as best you can, but allow God to do his perfect work in your Son's life.

Assignment: In your journal, finish the following sentences:

I am excited that I:

I am grateful for:

I believe that:

Thank you:

I need support in:

My next action step is:

Dr. Leslie Inspires Believes:

1. Mothers must create healthy boundaries for their Sons so they can live up to their full potential.

2. Self care must be prioritized to thrive.

3. When Mothers empower their Sons by giving them responsibility, they inspire them to be strong citizens in our society.

4. We compensate for our challenges by further strengthening our strengths.

5. Instead of complaining about what hasn't happened or what should be, we become the change we would like to see in the world and impact it accordingly.

6. Tune in to your "feeling of knowing" as intuition is a guide from God.

7. Obstacles are a fact of life. However, we do not allow them to pull us down, but to prepare us for the future.

8. Black women must raise their Sons to leave home and take care of their own family one day, not raise them to be dependent on others or other women.

9. Women have a responsibility to tend to their past and present in order to create a healthy future for themselves and their families.

10. We must be careful with the words we speak and think, as words manifest to be true. Positive affirmations can be sources of healing, strength, and inspiration.

About Dr. Leslie

Dr. Leslie, a former public school educator is the founder and CEO of Dr. Leslie Inspires, as well as Solid Foundation Christian Academy in Stone Mountain, Georgia. While working with families in public and private school settings for over 20+ years, Dr. Leslie has encountered many fragile relationships between African-American Mothers and their Sons. Between the raising of Black boys who find it difficult to become men to the boys who lack personal responsibility and end up in the US prison system, the need to help Black Mothers stop enabling their Sons and cultivate healthy relationships with them has become more clear. Since Dr. Leslie continues to see the same problem over and over again, she has developed a group coaching program and workshops to help women discover strategies to help their teen, twenty, thirty or forty something year old Son grow up? This problem did not just start. Dr. Leslie believes that if we empower and educate these struggling African-American Mothers then the boys to men cycle will be stronger and our young men will make better decisions.

Her book, *Setting Boundaries for Your African-American Son: 8 Steps to Taking Control of Your Life*, gives her a platform to help in a subject area that no one is talking about but everyone knows is true. She gets satisfaction and added-value to her life knowing she is making a difference in the lives of the people she serves. Being an agent for cultural change and seeing the impact she is having on Black Mothers and their Sons has put her on her soul's path. When someone that she has helped sees the impact that she has made in their life and comes back to say "thank you," it is her confirmation that she has stepped into her purpose for a time such as this. Dr. Leslie has a very distinct *"feeling of knowing"* that she is doing exactly what she was born to do at this point in her life. She believes that every experience and every conversation that she has had with a woman, a Black man, or Black youth was for now.

She believes that for the many personal, confidential, and emotional conversations that she has had with people, over the years, who believed, entrusted and sought out her advice...was for now.

THANK YOU!

Dr. Leslie Inspires offers ongoing workshops, seminars and retreats to help provide more support for those willing to do the work. We have candid discussions with other women who are also struggling with their Son and together we come up with other solutions. For more information on our workshops, seminars and retreats, please visit her online at www.drleslieinspires.com. She would love to hear more about the situation that you may be experiencing with your Son. Feel free to email me at info@drleslieinspires.com.

You can also:

1.   Schedule a Strategy Session with my team at calendly.com/drleslieinspires

2.   Show Up to the Strategy Session

3.   On your call, let the editor know you'd like us to send you a free copy of one of our books.

Made in the USA
San Bernardino, CA
23 October 2018